Kindergarten
MATH

WORKBOOK

Table of Contents:

COLOR AND TRACE

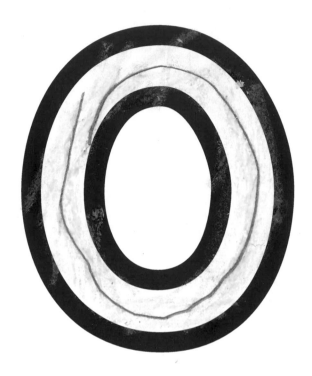

✏️ Trace the word **zero**.

zero zero zero

zero zero zero

Trace the number **0**.

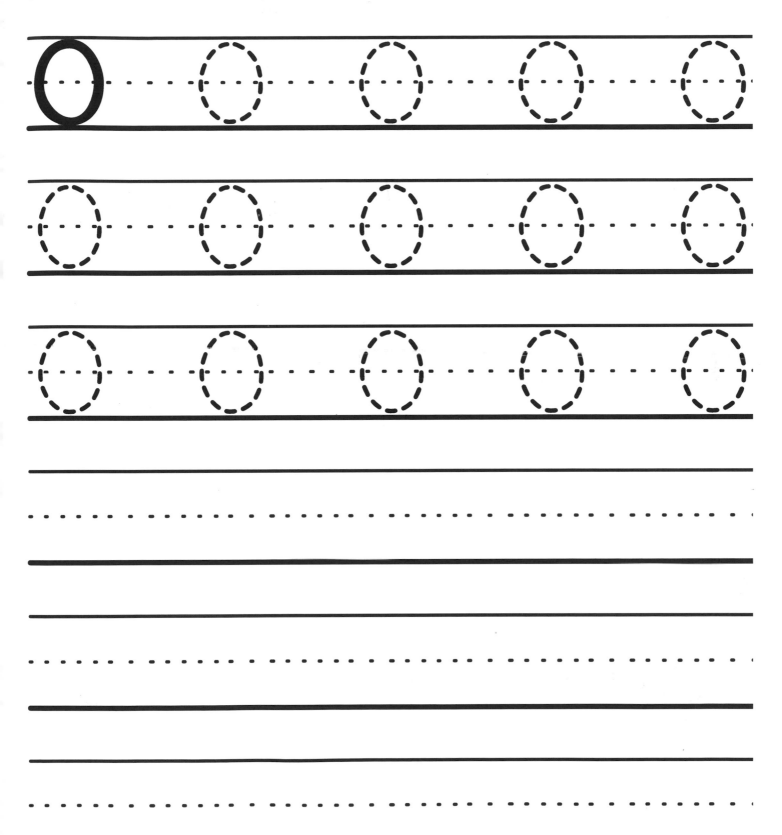

COLOR AND TRACE

✏️ Trace the word **one**.

one one one

one one one

✏️ Trace the number **1**.

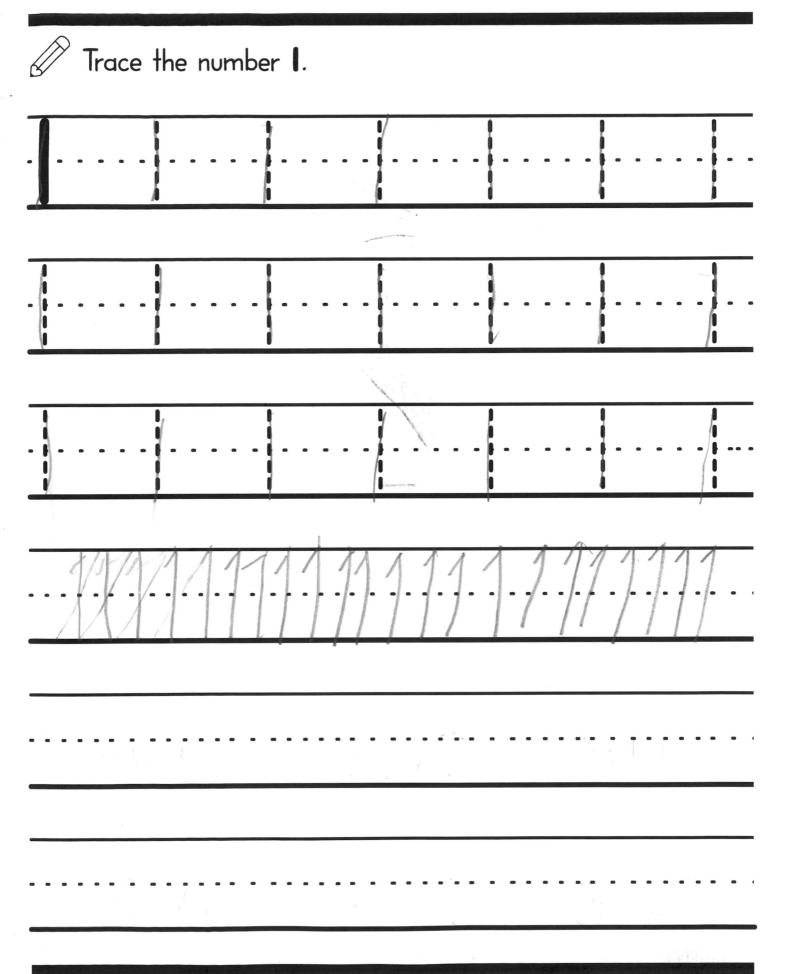

✏️ Trace the word **two**.

two two two

two two two

Trace the number **2**.

2 2 2 2 2

2 2 2 2 2

2 2 2 2 2

2 2 2 2 2 2 2 2 2

Trace the word **three**.

three   three

three   three

Trace the number **3**.

3 ---3--- ---3--- ---3--- ---3---

3 ---3--- ---3--- ---3--- ---3---

3 ---3--- ---3--- ---3--- ---3---

COLOR AND TRACE

✏️ Trace the word **four**.

four four four

four four four

Trace the number **4**.

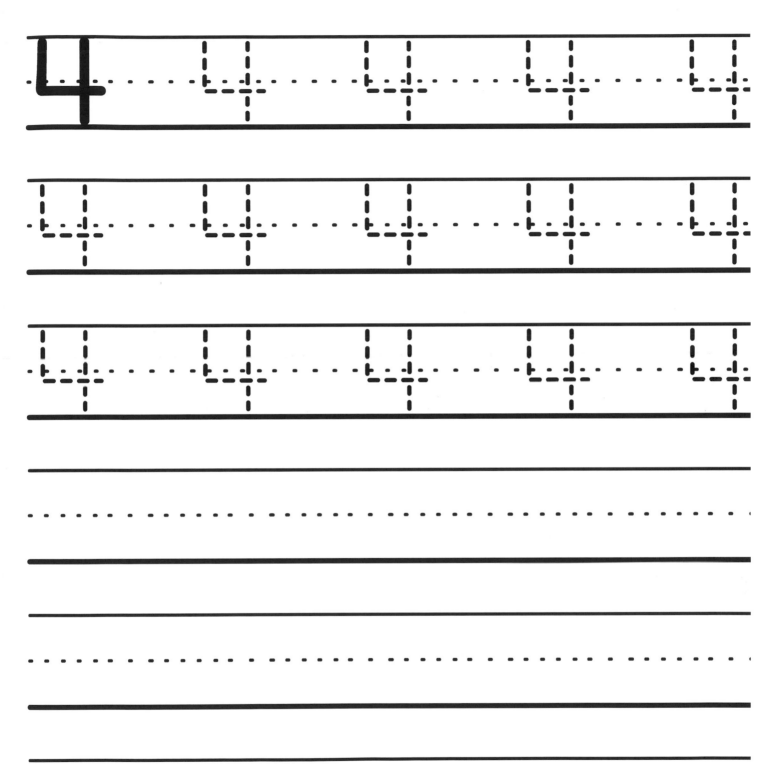

COLOR AND TRACE

Trace the word **five**.

five five five

five five five

Trace the number **5**.

5 5 5 5 5

5 5 5 5 5

5 5 5 5 5

 Trace the word **six**.

six   six   six   six

six   six   six   six

Trace the number **6**.

6   6   6   6   6

6   6   6   6   6

6   6   6   6   6

COLOR AND TRACE

 Trace the word **seven**.

seven ⠇seven

seven seven

Trace the number **7**.

7 7 7 7 7

7 7 7 7 7

7 7 7 7 7

✏️ Trace the word **eight**.

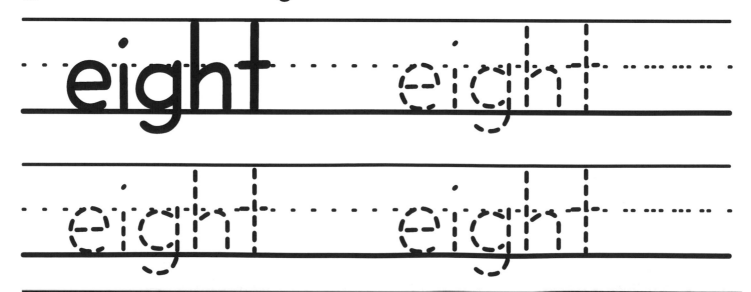

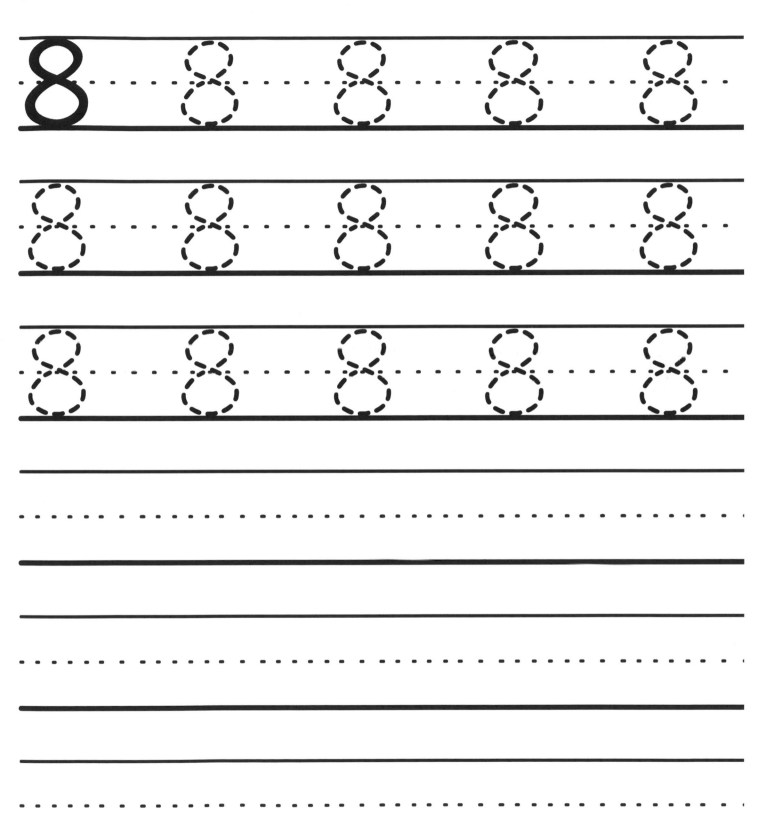

COLOR AND TRACE

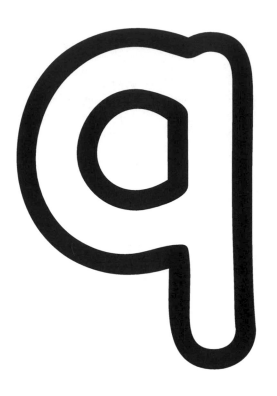

 Trace the word **nine**.

nine nine nine

nine nine nine

Trace the number **9**.

q

COLOR AND TRACE

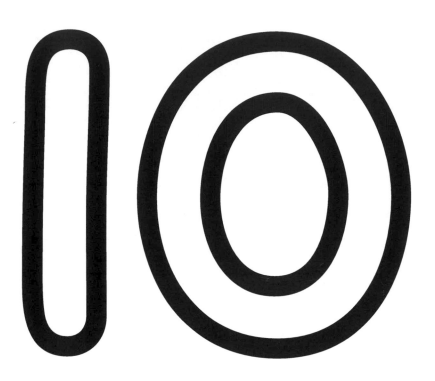

✏️ Trace the word **ten**.

ten ten ten ten

ten ten ten ten

Trace the number **10**.

10 · · · 1O · · · 1O · · · 1O

1O · · · 1O · · · 1O · · · 1O

1O · · · 1O · · · 1O · · · 1O

Count the dots and fill in the missing numbers.

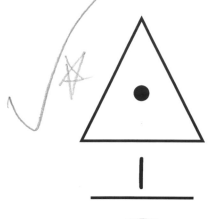 1

 2

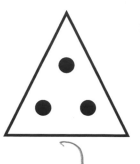 3

 4

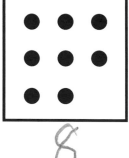 5

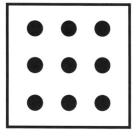 6

 7

 8

 9

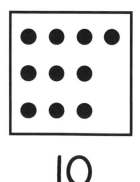 10

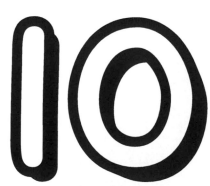

More

 Which has more? Circle the picture and then write the numbers.

There are more

| 4 | is more than | |

There are more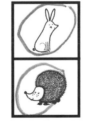

| 6 | is more than | 5 |

The number 4 comes **between** 3 and 5.

3 4 5

 Write the number that comes **between** these numbers.

1 2 3

7 8 9

8 9 10

Less

 Which has less? Circle the picture and then write the numbers.

There are less

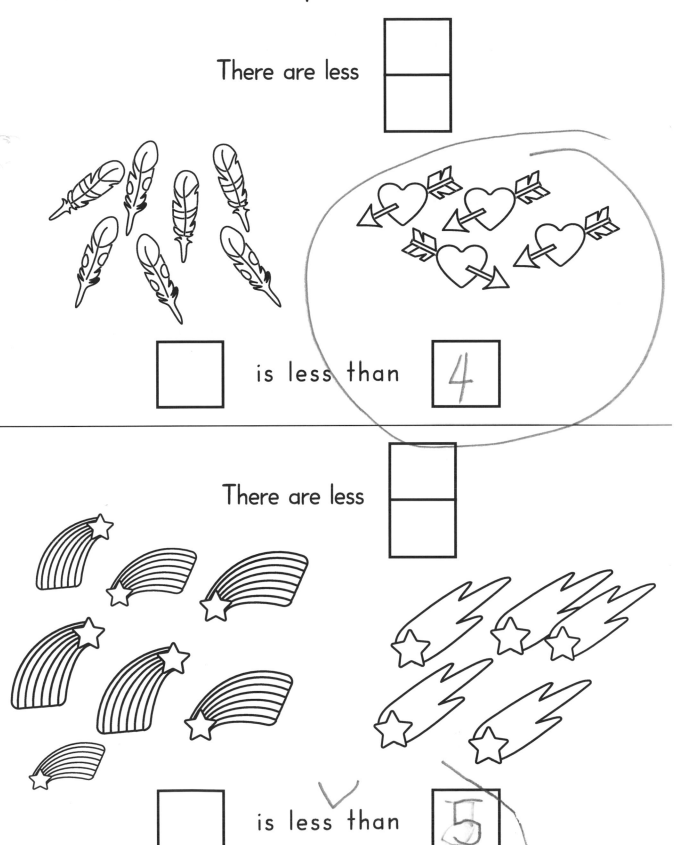

There are less [ ]

[ ] is less than [4]

There are less [ ]

[ ] is less than [5]

31

Less

 Which has less? Write how many in each box and then color the picture that has less.

How many?

5

How many?

6

☐ is less than ☐

The number 5 comes **after** 3, 4.

3 4 ᠁5᠁

 Write the number that comes **after** these numbers.

2 3 _____

8 9 _____

5 6 _____

How many ⊕ do you see? ☐

How many ◺ do you see? ☐

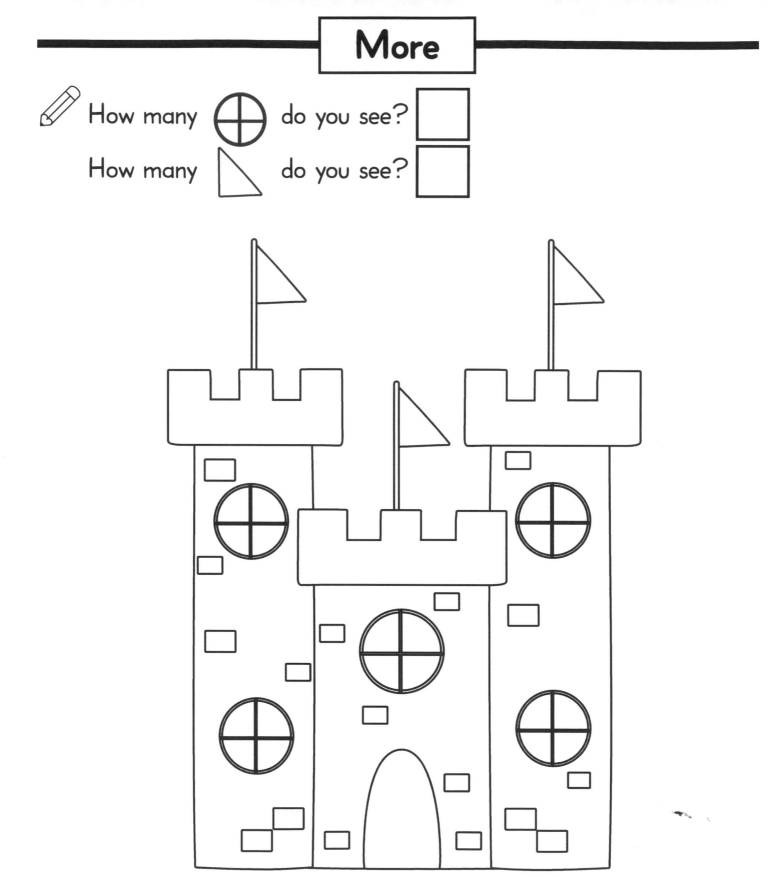

Are there more or ? Circle your answer.

The number 6 comes **before** 7, 8.

 Write the number that comes **before** these numbers.

$$3 \quad 4$$

$$8 \quad 9$$

$$6 \quad 7$$

Circle 10 things and then write the numbers.

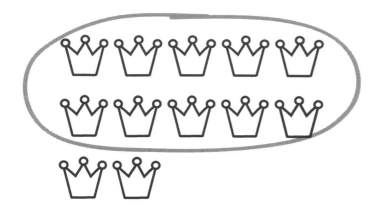

| 10 | and | 2 |

☐ and ☐

☐ and ☐

☐ and ☐

Circle 10 things and then write the numbers.

☐ and ☐

☐ and ☐

☐ and ☐

☐ and ☐

Count by 2's

 Write in each missing number to count by 2's.

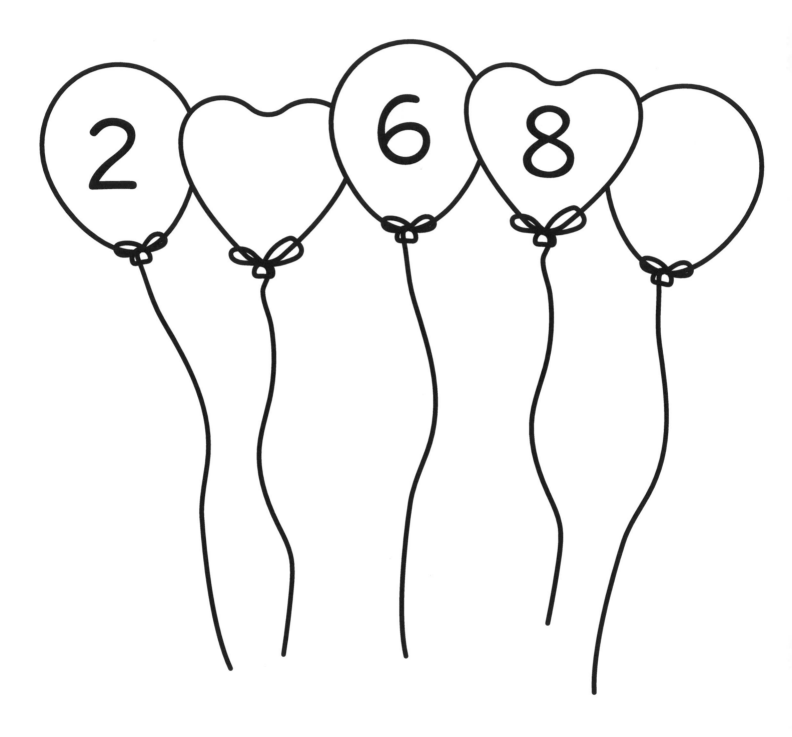

I can count by 2's!

Make 10

 Fill in the blank circles to make 10!

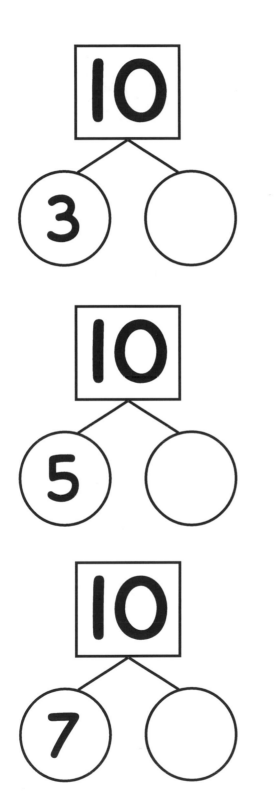

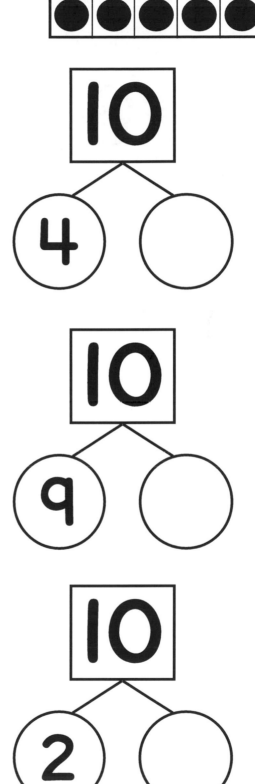

Make 6

Fill in the blank circles to make 6!

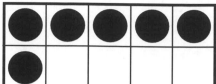

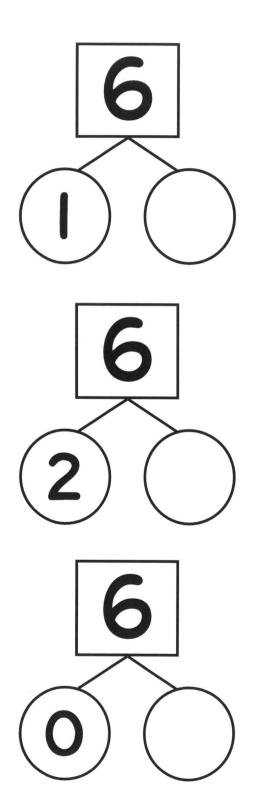

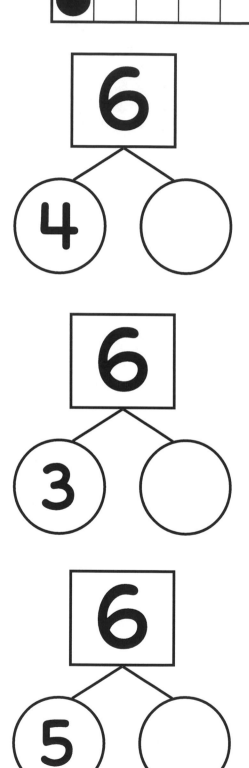

Make 8

 Fill in the blank circles to make 8!

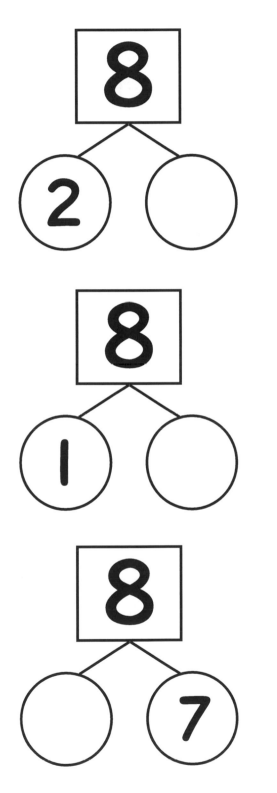

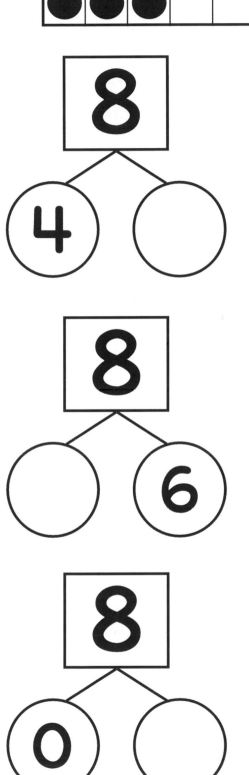

Fill in the blank boxes to make 10!

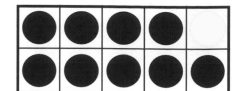

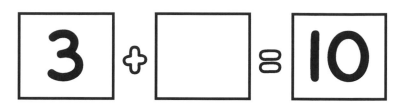

$$3 + \boxed{} = 10$$

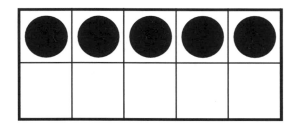

$$5 + \boxed{} = 10$$

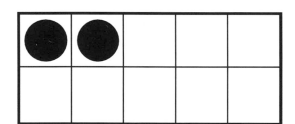

$$2 + \boxed{} = 10$$

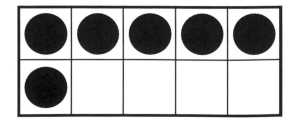

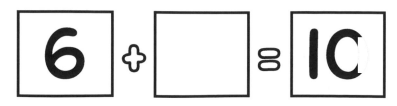

$$6 + \boxed{} = 10$$

Write the numbers.

| 1 | + | 4 | = | |

| 2 | + | 5 | = | |

| 6 | + | 3 | = | |

| 8 | + | 1 | = | |

Make 10

 Fill in the blank boxes to make 10!

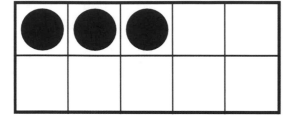

$3 + \boxed{} = 10$

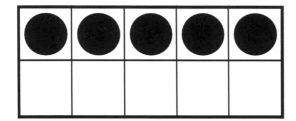

$5 + \boxed{} = 10$

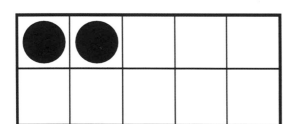

$2 + \boxed{} = 10$

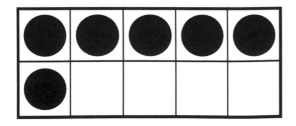

$6 + \boxed{} = 10$

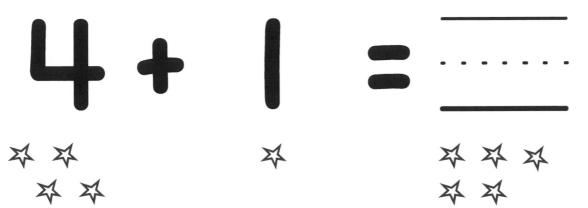

4 + 1 = _____

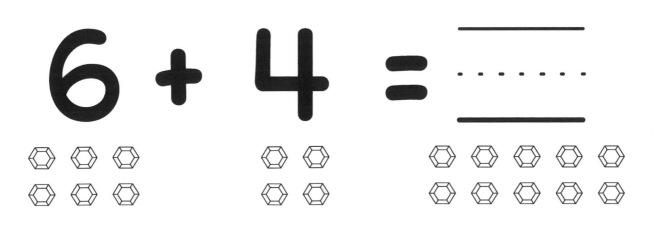

3 + 5 = _____

6 + 4 = _____

Fill in the blank boxes to make 10!

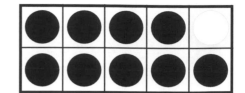

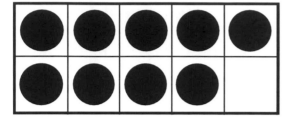

$$9 + \boxed{} = 10$$

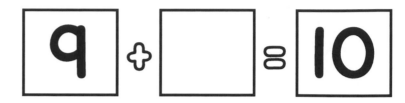

$$4 + \boxed{} = 10$$

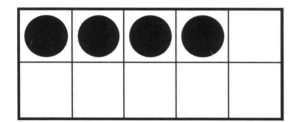

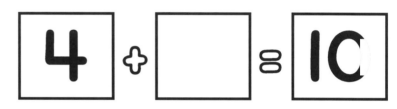

$$7 + \boxed{} = 10$$

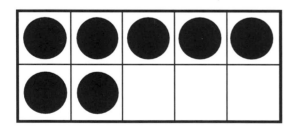

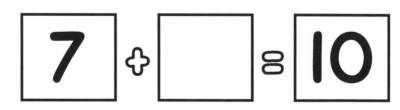

$$8 + \boxed{} = 10$$

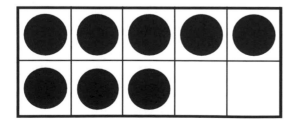

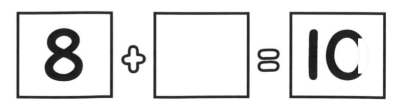

Addition

 Write the numbers.

| 1 | + | 4 | = | |

| 2 | + | 5 | = | |

| 6 | + | 3 | = | |

| 8 | + | 1 | = | |

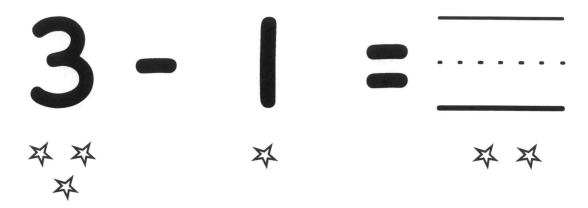

$3 - 1 =$ _____

$5 - 3 =$ _____

$7 - 4 =$ _____

Write the numbers.

Bear and Fox went into the woods

to gather for dinner.

Bear ate .

There is still ☐ left for Fox.

☐ - ☐ = ☐

Hippo and Turtle went to the lake

to hunt for for a snack.

Hippo ate  .

There are still ☐ left for Turtle.

☐ - ☐ = ☐

6 - 3 = ...

9 - 6 = ...

8 - 1 = ...

Write the numbers.

Sparkle and Shimmer went to the store

to buy for their friends.

They gave away.

There are still ☐ left for Sparkle and Shimmer.

☐ - ☐ = ☐

Twilight and Twinkle went to the candy store

to buy for their friends.

Twilight & Twinkle ate on the way home.

There are still ☐ left for their friends.

☐ - ☐ = ☐

COLOR AND TRACE

✏️ Trace the word **eleven**.

eleven eleven

eleven eleven

Trace the number **11**.

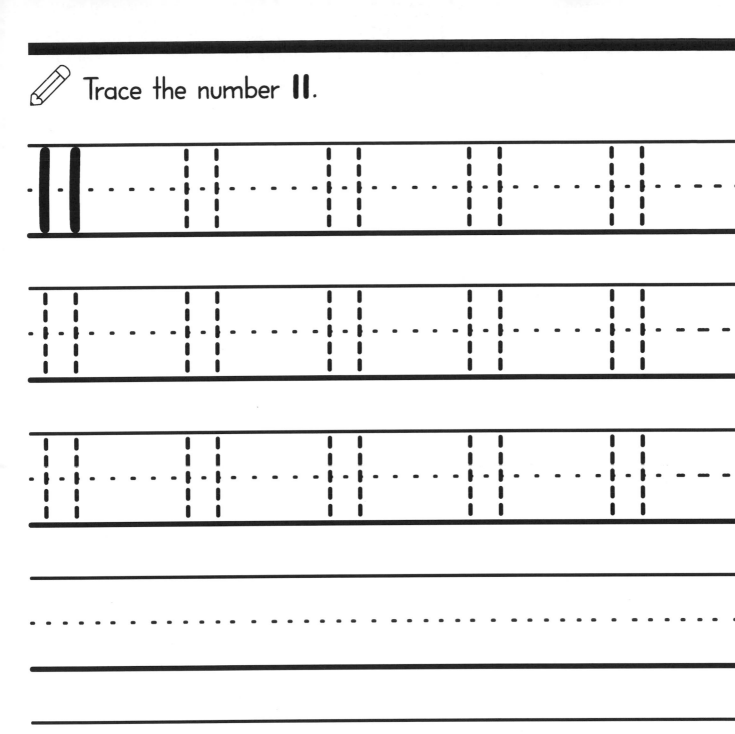

COLOR AND TRACE

✏️ Trace the word **twelve**.

twelve   twelve

twelve   twelve

Trace the number **12**.

12 ¦2 ¦2 ¦2

¦2 ¦2 ¦2 ¦2

¦2 ¦2 ¦2 ¦2

COLOR AND TRACE

✏️ Trace the word **thirteen**.

thirteen thirteen

thirteen thirteen

Trace the number **13**.

13 13 13 13

13 13 13 13

13 13 13 13

COLOR AND TRACE

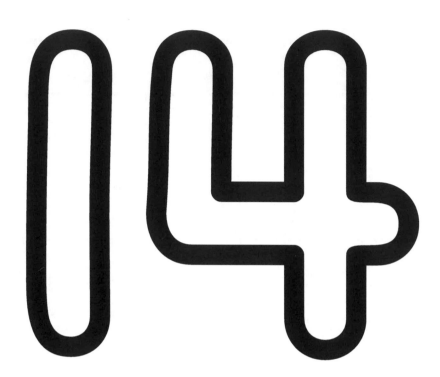

✏️ Trace the word **fourteen**.

fourteen fourteen

fourteen fourteen

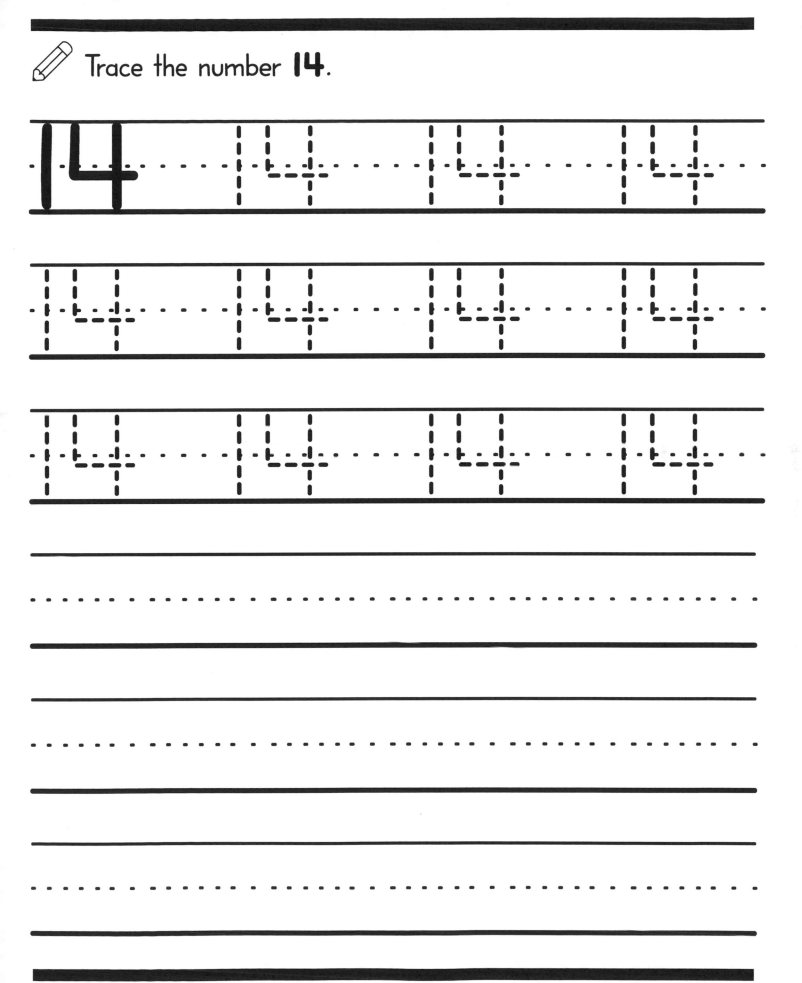

Trace the number **14**.

COLOR AND TRACE

 Trace the word **fifteen**.

fifteen   fifteen

fifteen   fifteen

15   15   15   15

15   15   15   15

15   15   15   15

COLOR AND TRACE

 Trace the word **sixteen**.

sixteen sixteen

sixteen sixteen

16   16   16   16

16   16   16   16

16   16   16   16

COLOR AND TRACE

✏️ Trace the word **seventeen**.

seventeen

seventeen

Trace the number **17**.

17 17 17 17

17 17 17 17

17 17 17 17

COLOR AND TRACE

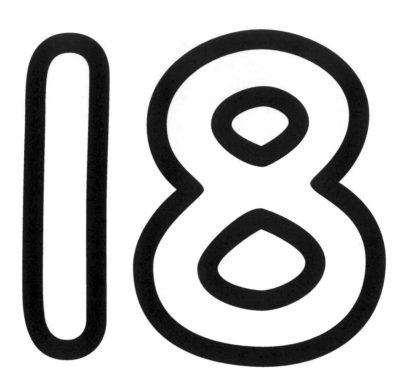

✏️ Trace the word **eighteen**.

eighteen eighteen

eighteen eighteen

Trace the number **18**.

18 18 18 18

18 18 18 18

18 18 18 18

COLOR AND TRACE

Trace the word **nineteen**.

nineteen nineteen

nineteen nineteen

Trace the number **19**.

19   19   19   19

19   19   19   19

19   19   19   19

COLOR AND TRACE

20

Trace the word **twenty**.

twenty ⋯ twenty

twenty ⋯ twenty

Trace the number **20**.

20   20   20

20   20   20

20   20   20

Color the ◇ blue.
Color the ◯ yellow.

Are there fewer ◇ or ◯ ?
Circle your answer.

✏️ Color the △ blue.

Color the ◯ yellow.

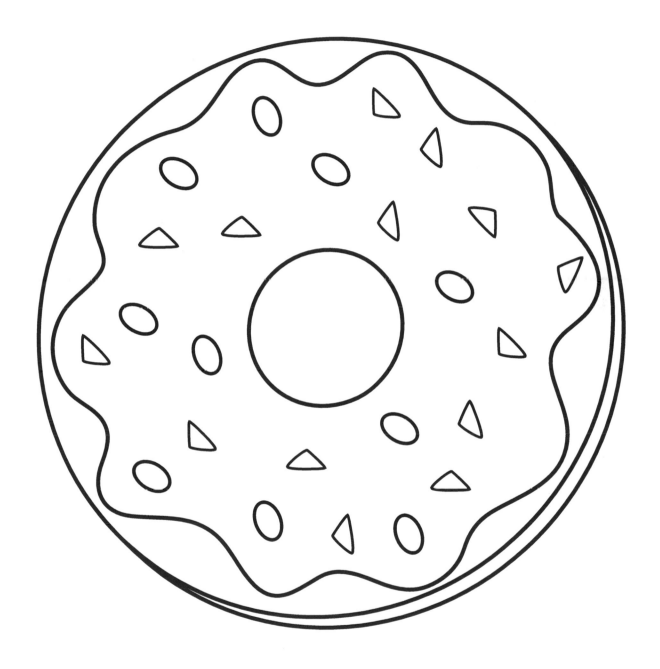

✏️ Are there more △ sprinkles or ◯ dots?
Circle your answer.

Make 20

 Fill in the blank circles to make 20!

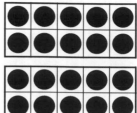

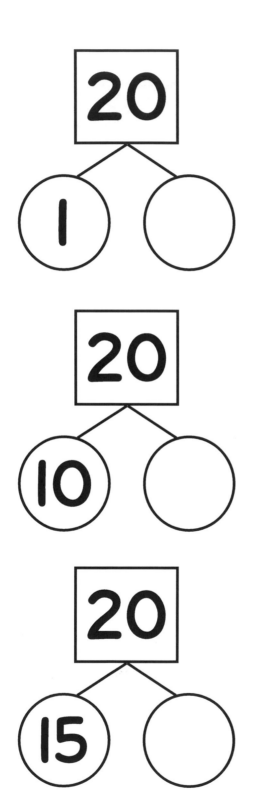

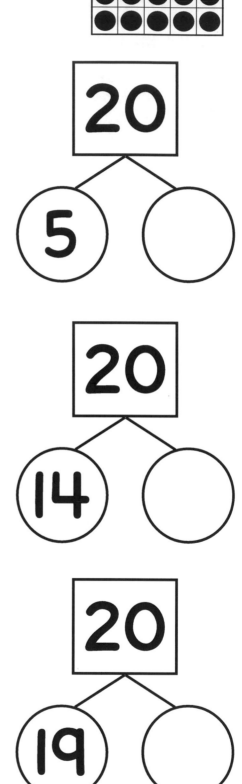

74

Count by 2's

 Write in each missing number to count by 2's.

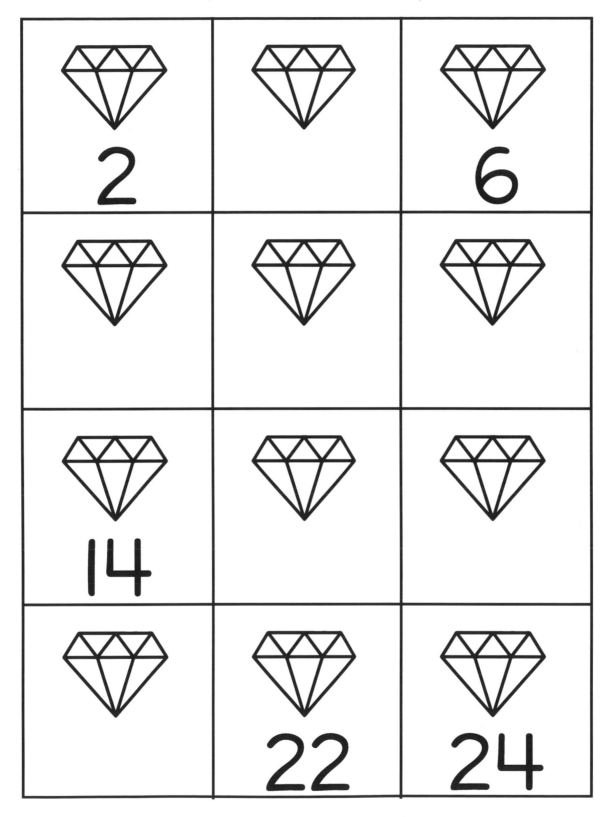

I can count by 2's!

Fill in the blank boxes to make 20.

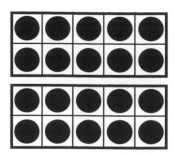

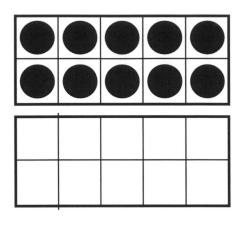

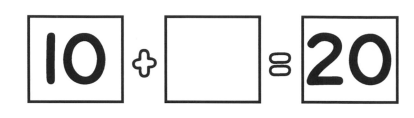
$10 + \boxed{} = 20$

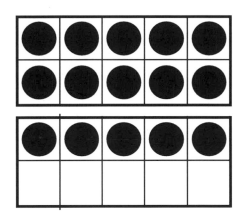

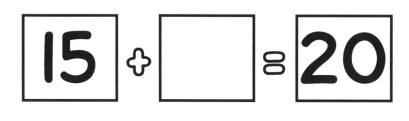
$15 + \boxed{} = 20$

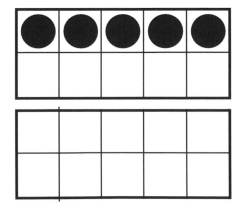

$5 + \boxed{} = 20$

Make 20

 Fill in the blank boxes to make 20.

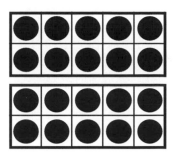

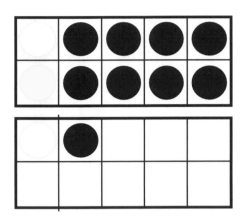   12 + ▢ = 20

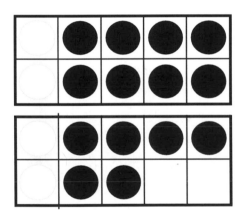   18 + ▢ = 20

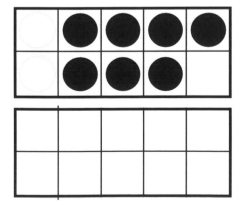   9 + ▢ = 20

Trace the numbers on the clock to complete the picture.

Tell the time by writing the numbers.

      o'clock

   o'clock

   o'clock

Time

 Draw the two hands of the clock to write the time on the right.

Time

 Write the correct time in each clock on the right.

 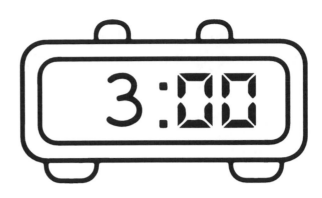

100
one hundred

✏️ Point to each number as you count to 100.

100 gold stars for you... YOU DID IT!

Count by 5's

 Write in each missing number to count by 5's.

5   15

            35

                  60

            75

      90   100

I can count by 5's!

Write in each missing number to count by 10's to 100.

	20
30	
	80
90	

I can count by 10's!

Count the shapes and write the number in each box.

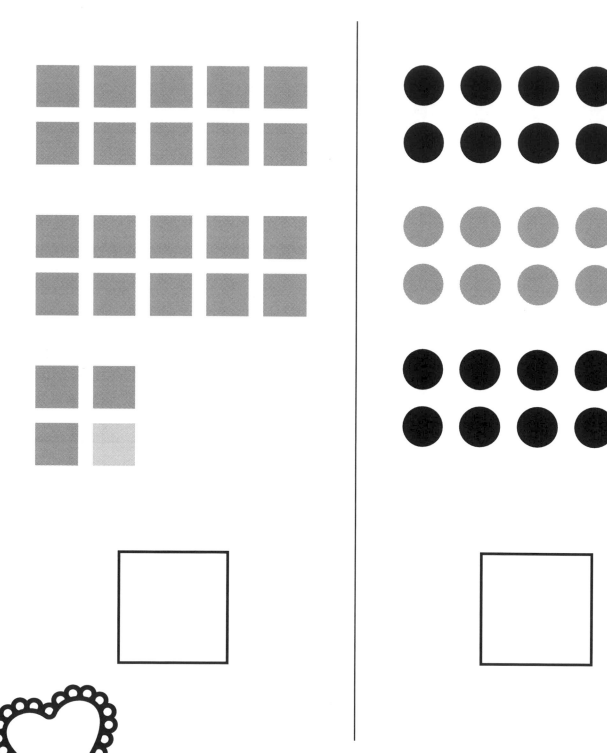

Count

Count the shapes and write the number in each box.

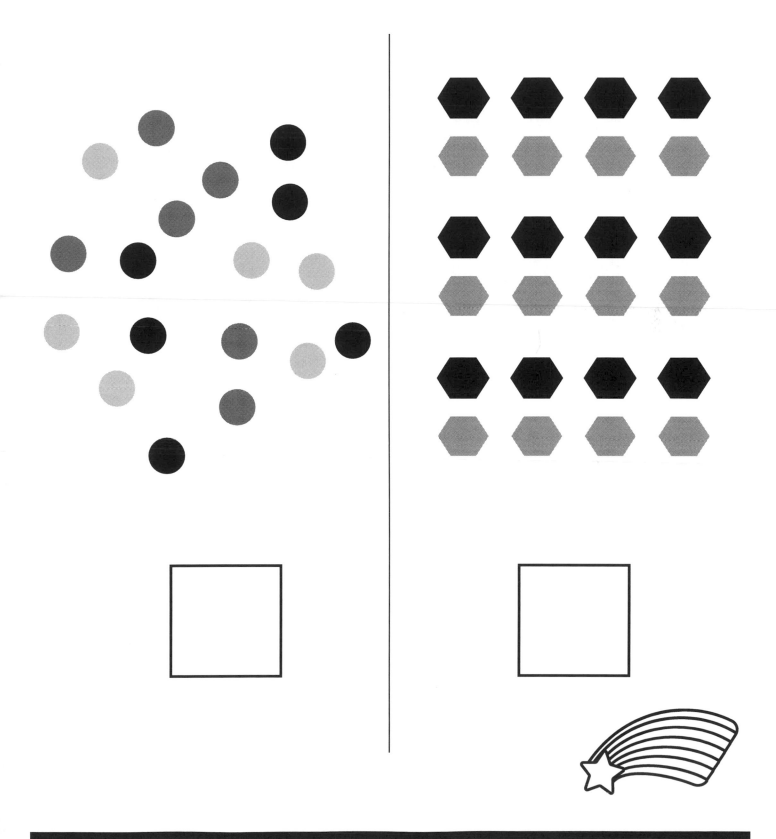

Color each coin.

penny
1 cent

nickel
5 cents

dime
10 cents

quarter
25 cents

Money

Draw a line to match each coin with the correct amount.

10 cents

5 cents

1 cent

25 cents

Write the amount.

A **penny** is

☐ cent.

• •

 Add up the pennies then write the amount.

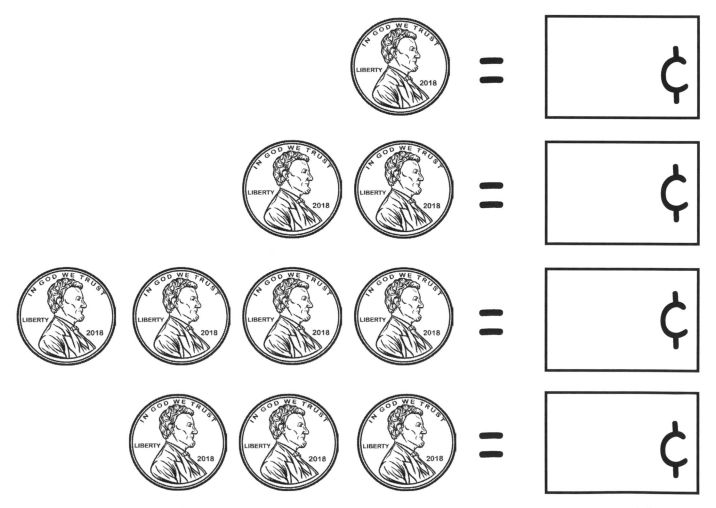

Write the amount.

A **nickel** is

☐ cents.

· ·

 Add up the nickels then write the amount.

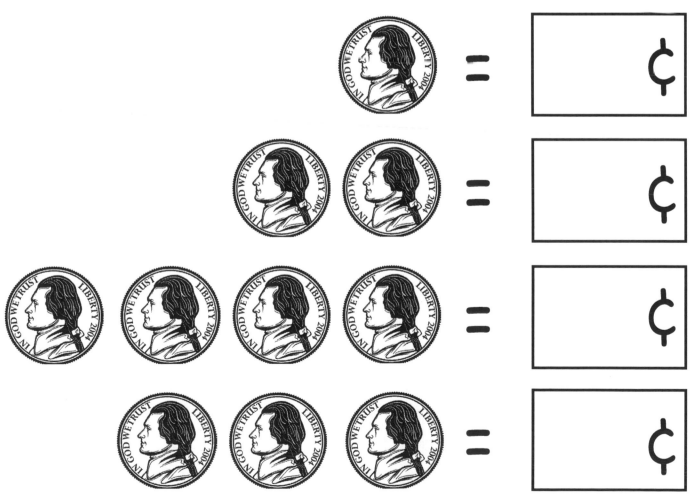

Write the amount.

A **dime** is

 cents.

 Add up the dimes then write the amount.

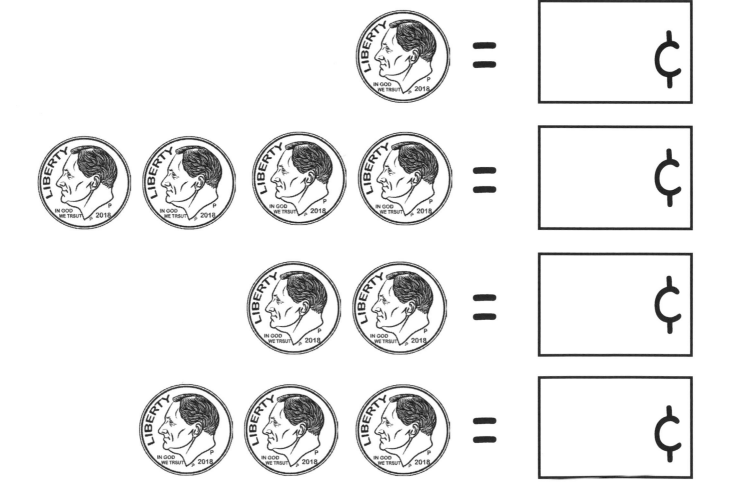

Write the amount.

A **quarter** is

☐ cents.

• •

 Add up the quarters then write the amount.

    =  ¢

  =  ¢

  =  ¢

 =  ¢

Color the correct coin to pay for the ice cream.

 1¢

 25¢

 5¢

 10¢